VOTING ISSUES
OF TODAY

BY CYNTHIA KENNEDY HENZEL

CONTENT CONSULTANT
ROBERT Y. SHAPIRO, PhD
PROFESSOR OF POLITICAL SCIENCE AND INTERNATIONAL AND
PUBLIC AFFAIRS
COLUMBIA UNIVERSITY

Essential Library

An Imprint of Abdo Publishing | abdobooks.com

abdobooks.com

Published by Abdo Publishing, a division of ABDO, PO Box 398166, Minneapolis, Minnesota 55439. Copyright © 2021 by Abdo Consulting Group, Inc. International copyrights reserved in all countries. No part of this book may be reproduced in any form without written permission from the publisher. Essential Library™ is a trademark and logo of Abdo Publishing.

Printed in the United States of America, North Mankato, Minnesota.
102020
012021

Cover Photo: Chuck Nacke/Alamy
Interior Photos: Keith Srakocic/AP Images, 4–5; Adam Kaz/iStockphoto, 7; Everett Collection/Shutterstock Images, 11; North Wind Picture Archives, 14–15; Pat Benic/ UPI/Newscom, 16; Library of Congress, 21; Atlanta Journal-Constitution/AP Images, 24; David Goldman/AP Images, 26–27; John Minchillo/AP Images, 32; Marcio Jose Sanchez/AP Images, 34; Matt Rourke/AP Images, 38; Rogelio V. Solis/AP Images, 41; Charles Krupa/AP Images, 42–43; Rebekah Zemansky/Shutterstock Images, 47; Rob Crandall/Shutterstock Images, 50–51; Seth Wenig/AP Images, 57; John Raoux/ AP Images, 60–61, 83; Tom Williams/CQ Roll Call/Newscom, 65; Carolyn Kaster/AP Images, 68–69; Steve Helber/AP Images, 71; Deepak Sethi/iStockphoto, 76; John Locher/AP Images, 78–79, 94; Bill Clark/CQ Roll Call/AP Images, 85; Pablo Martinez Monsivais/AP Images, 88–89; Ross D. Franklin/AP Images, 90–91; Andree Kehn/Sun Journal/AP Images, 97

Editor: Charly Haley
Series Designer: Maggie Villaume

Library of Congress Control Number: 2020940295

Publisher's Cataloging-in-Publication Data

Names: Henzel, Cynthia Kennedy, author.
Title: Voting issues of today / by Cynthia Kennedy Henzel
Description: Minneapolis, Minnesota : Abdo Publishing, 2021 | Series: Special reports
        | Includes online resources and index
Identifiers: ISBN 9781532194177 (lib. bdg.) | ISBN 9781098213534 (ebook)
Subjects: LCSH: Voting--Juvenile literature. | Absentee voting--United States--
        Juvenile literature. | Voter turnout--Juvenile literature. | Presidential
        candidates--United States--Juvenile literature. | Right and left (Political
        science)--Juvenile literature. | Political parties--Platforms--Juvenile literature.
Classification: DDC 324.6--dc23

CONTENTS

A COMPLEX
SYSTEM

T hings changed for Alfonzo Tucker Jr. when his 18-year-old son tried to register to vote. In response to filling out the form, his son received a letter from the state of Alabama saying he was ineligible to vote. To Tucker, this didn't make sense. His family had lived in Alabama his whole life. His son had never been in trouble with the law. Why couldn't he vote?

Tucker himself had not been able to vote for years. In the 1980s, he was convicted of third-degree assault, a misdemeanor, for a fight at a club. Then, in the 1990s, he was convicted of second-degree assault, a felony, for a fight with a police officer. He was sent to prison for two years, then served some time on probation.

There are many volunteer organizations with the goal of helping people register to vote.

Tucker became more mature while in prison. After he got out, he found a job and had children. However, he could not vote because felons in Alabama lose their right to vote.

While Tucker was in prison, he had read about Black Americans fighting in the 1960s against discriminatory policies that blocked their right to vote. Tucker decided voting was worth fighting for. Under Alabama law, felons could apply to regain their voting rights but not until they served their time in prison and paid all the fees they owed to the state. Tucker worked to pay down the $1,600 in court fees he owed so he could vote.

Although Tucker had never voted before he went to jail, he began voting once he regained the right to do so. He and his wife would take their two young children into the voting

MARTIN LUTHER KING JR.

Martin Luther King Jr. led the civil rights movement from the 1950s until his assassination in 1968. He promoted nonviolent protest to end segregation in the United States. This fight was especially important in the South, where Jim Crow laws required white people and Black people to be separated in nearly all public spaces. In March 1965, King organized protesters in Selma, Alabama, to promote the need for a federal voting rights law that banned states from discriminating against Black voters. After Alabama state troopers violently stopped the marchers with batons and tear gas, King led a second march of 1,500 people to the Edmund Pettus Bridge outside Selma. When troopers lined up to block the march, the protesters knelt in prayer, then turned back. Although King received some criticism for being too cautious, many say the Voting Rights Act of 1965 passed largely as a result of his work.

Voting for the first time is exciting for many young people.

booth with them to teach them how important voting was. Then in 2013, Tucker got a letter from the state of Alabama saying he could not vote again. He didn't know why, and the letter didn't explain how he could get his voting rights back. Tucker decided to let it go.

Several years later, Tucker's son, Alfonzo Tucker III, got the letter saying he could not vote. The family eventually discovered this was a mix-up because Tucker and his son shared a name. The issue was fixed, and Tucker's son was able to register and vote. But helping his son get registered made Tucker decide that he wanted to get back his own right to vote. He had canvassed the year before for

Democrat Doug Jones for US Senate. He wanted to vote for Walt Maddox, the former mayor of his hometown of Tuscaloosa, for governor.

In 2018, Tucker called the Alabama Board of Pardons and Paroles, the agency in charge of restoring voting rights. Two weeks later, he got a letter from the board saying he could not register to vote because he still owed $135.10 in fees. Tucker borrowed the money and paid the state. He was then told that he owed another $5,535.47 from an older conviction. Tucker didn't understand why he kept getting new bills, so he contacted an attorney from a nonprofit voting rights group.

The attorney found that Tucker had not owed the $135.10 because it was not directly related to his conviction. Plus, the attorney discovered that the $5,535.47

DISCRIMINATORY VOTING LAWS

In the early 1900s, and long afterwards, many states created laws to suppress Black Americans' right to vote. These included literacy tests targeting Black Americans who didn't have access to education and poll taxes that many Black Americans could not afford. In 1901, Alabama leaders passed a law mandating that people convicted of certain felony crimes lose the right to vote. The law was targeted at Black Americans, who were disproportionately convicted due to long-standing discrimination in the US criminal justice system. John Knox, who helped pass the law as president of the Alabama Constitutional Convention, said, "If we would have white supremacy, we must establish it by law—not by force or fraud."[1]

was for a conviction of a misdemeanor, which did not affect Tucker's legal right to vote. All Tucker owed to be able to vote was $4.00. However, it took so long for Tucker to get the mistakes cleared up that he did not get to vote in the 2018 election.[2]

VOTING LAWS

Voting is the defining right of a democracy. Without the right to vote for leaders and laws, citizens have little say in how the government is run. But voting in the United States is a complex system. Each state and territory of the country has its own voting laws that determine who can register to vote and how those people can register. States draw their own lines to create voting districts.

States also determine the number and placement of polling precincts. They decide what time the polls open

THE AMERICAN CIVIL LIBERTIES UNION

The American Civil Liberties Union (ACLU) was founded by lawyers in 1920 to protect people in the United States who had their civil rights violated by the government. The ACLU has argued in court for the rights of all voters to get access to the ballot. It has advocated against laws aimed at putting limitations on certain groups of voters. In 2020, during the COVID-19 pandemic, the ACLU fought to ensure that people could vote safely by mail-in ballot to protect themselves and others during the 2020 presidential election. Several states began to allow mail-in ballots for all voters.

and close. They decide whether votes are cast on paper, electronically, or both. States make laws about whether voters can use mail-in ballots or vote early ahead of Election Day.

States also differ on laws regarding state primary elections and caucuses, which political parties use to nominate candidates to run in general elections. States determine who can vote in primaries. They choose how referendums, or political questions decided directly by voters, can be placed on the ballot. While federal law guarantees citizens the right to vote, the way in which people can exercise this right is determined by various state laws.

VOTING ISSUES

Voting has had many issues to overcome since the beginning of the United States. The government has ratified four amendments to the US Constitution concerning who may vote. For example, the Fifteenth Amendment gave black men the right to vote in 1870.

Some of the most powerful citizen movements have centered around voting rights. Women gained the right to vote in 1920 as a result of the women's suffrage movement. But even then, most Black women still could not vote due to state laws. Various state laws blocked many Black people from voting until the 1960s. State laws about voting can frequently change. Throughout US history, some laws have been designed to ensure

The Fifteenth Amendment changed federal law, giving Black men the right to vote in every state. Before the amendment passed, only a small number of states had laws allowing Black men to vote.

MORE TO THE
STORY

WAR OF THE ROSES

The US women's suffrage movement began in 1848 when Elizabeth Cady Stanton and Lucretia Mott led the Seneca Falls Convention in New York. The convention was organized to demand voting rights for women. In January 1918, President Woodrow Wilson said he supported a constitutional amendment to give women the right to vote. The next year, the US Congress passed the Nineteenth Amendment to give women the right to vote, but amendments must also be ratified by three-fourths of the states to become part of the Constitution. At the time, that meant 36 states. By March 1920, 35 states had ratified the amendment, seven had opposed it, and the decision came down to Tennessee. The battle became known as the War of the Roses. Those in favor of ratification wore yellow roses, and those opposed wore red. The Tennessee Senate voted in favor of the amendment, but the Tennessee House of Representatives was divided 48 to 48. The Speaker of the House called for a vote on ratification. Representative Harry Burn, wearing a red rose but clutching a letter from his mother, changed his vote to yes. The resolution passed, and the Nineteenth Amendment became law. The next day, Burn explained, "I know that a mother's advice is always safest for her boy to follow, and my mother wanted me to vote for ratification."[3]

the right to vote, and others have been designed to suppress voting.

Some issues in the American voting system have arisen from people in power wanting to suppress the vote in a way that helps them remain in power. Some voting issues

have arisen from those with money, such as powerful industries or interest groups, wanting the government to pass legislation in their favor. Other issues have stemmed from a lack of clarity over how much power the federal government has over states to determine voting laws.

Voting issues also arise because of people who don't vote. Some people don't vote because they have little trust in the government or because they believe their vote doesn't matter. Others don't vote because they don't want to take the time and effort to learn about the candidates, register to vote, or cast a ballot. But for many people in the United States, voting matters.

HISTORY OF AMERICAN VOTING

To understand the voting issues of today, it is necessary to understand the laws that control voting in the United States. The US Constitution, which went into effect in 1789, set up how the president, the vice president, and the members of Congress are elected. However, since the ratification of the Constitution, those processes have changed.

Members of the US Senate were originally elected by the state legislatures. That changed for all states in 1913 with the Seventeenth Amendment. Since then, the two senators that represent each state have been elected directly by the people in the state.

The Founding Fathers of the United States put together the US Constitution at the Constitutional Convention in 1787.

The people in each state have always directly elected members of the House of Representatives. States have different numbers of representatives depending on their populations. The Constitution mandated at least one representative per state and no more than one for every 30,000 people. Every ten years, the US Census determines the population of each state. The House reapportions itself, and states with more people are given more representatives.

However, as the population of the country grew, the number of representatives kept increasing. To solve the problem of having an unmanageably high number of representatives, the House passed the Permanent Apportionment Act of 1929. This capped the number of

The House of Representatives meets in the US Capitol in Washington, DC.

representatives at 435, which was the total number of representatives after the 1910 census reapportionment. Today, reapportionment still happens after the Census every ten years. States that lose population may lose representatives, and states that have increased population may gain representatives, but the total remains at 435.

THE ELECTORAL COLLEGE

The president is not elected directly by the citizens of the United States. He or she is elected by a group called the electoral college, which is made up of electors from the states. Originally, state legislatures chose the electors, but today, the electors are chosen by voters. The number of electors in each state is equal to the state's number of senators, which is always two, plus its number of US representatives, which changes based on population. There is a minimum of three electors per state. Washington, DC, also has three electors. US territories, such as Puerto Rico and Guam, do not have electors as their citizens do not vote in presidential elections.

Candidates for president and vice president run together on a party ticket. The electors choose the

MORE TO THE
STORY

THE POWER
OF ELECTORS

In July 2020, the US Supreme Court ruled that states have the power to require their members of the electoral college to vote for the candidate who wins the popular vote in their state. Electors usually vote for the candidate who wins the popular vote—but not always. Some electors, known as faithless electors, have voted for other candidates. Ten electors in 2016 voted or tried to vote for candidates who did not win the popular vote in their states.[1] Although this did not change the result of the 2016 election because the race wasn't close enough for it to make a difference, an equal number of faithless electors could have changed the results of five previous presidential elections.

People who support faithless electors often believe that the founders of the US Constitution intended electors to vote independently, just as elected members of Congress vote on bills independently. Meanwhile, people who say electors should represent their state's popular vote often believe that because the power to choose electors was originally given to state legislatures, states should be able to make electors follow the vote of the people. At the time of the July 2020 Supreme Court ruling, some states already had laws requiring electors to follow the popular vote, so the court's ruling reaffirmed those laws as constitutional.

winning candidates after the general public votes in the November election. Each state legislature determines how the state's electoral votes are assigned from its state's popular vote. All of the states except Maine and Nebraska have a winner-take-all system. Winner-take-all means all electors from a state are supposed to vote for whoever received the most votes in the state during the November election. In Maine and Nebraska, two electoral votes always go to the winner of the state's popular vote, while the rest of the electors are divided based on who wins the popular vote in each district.

VICE PRESIDENT

The process of electing a vice president of the United States has changed several times. The original US Constitution made the runner-up in the presidential election the vice president. This did not work well, since the two people taking the top votes might have very different ideas about running the country. Under the Twelfth Amendment, ratified in 1804, the process was changed so that electors voted for a president and vice president separately. Today, presidential candidates for each party pick a running mate, or a person to run for vice president. A presidential candidate and his or her running mate then campaign together, appear on ballots together, and can only be elected together. The process to fill a vacancy in the office of vice president has also changed. Although the US Constitution explained that the vice president would take on presidential duties if the president were unable to serve, it did not provide a successor to the vice presidency. Therefore, if the office of vice president became vacant, it remained vacant until the next election. The Twenty-Fifth Amendment clarified that the vice president automatically becomes president if the president resigns or dies, and it gave the president the power to nominate someone to fill the office of vice president. His or her nominee must then be approved by Congress.

NATIVE AMERICAN AND ASIAN VOTERS

In 1876, a federal court ruled that Native Americans were not US citizens under the Fourteenth Amendment. This meant they did not have the right to vote. Congress passed the Dawes Act in 1886, providing a pathway for Native Americans to apply for US citizenship if they renounced their tribal citizenship. Then in 1924, the Indian Citizenship Act gave all Native Americans US citizenship. However, some state laws still kept many Native Americans from voting. This included laws requiring competency tests and laws disallowing people who lived on reservations to vote. Utah became the last state to remove these barriers in 1962.

Asian Americans were also denied citizenship. The Naturalization Act of 1790 stated that only "free white citizens of good character" could become naturalized citizens.[3] The Chinese Exclusion Act of 1882 explicitly forbade Chinese immigrants from becoming US citizens. Finally, the McCarran-Walter Act of 1952 allowed Asian immigrants to become citizens and vote.

THE RIGHT TO VOTE

According to the US Constitution, laws regarding how elections are held and who can vote are the responsibility of the states. In 1789, only 6 percent of people in the new United States of America were eligible to vote for the first president, George Washington.[2] At that time, states legislated that voters had to be white men who were at least 21 years old and owned property.

Over time, states dropped the requirement for owning property. By 1856, all white men could vote. Some states, such as Wyoming starting in 1890, allowed women to vote. But it took amendments to the Constitution to expand voting rights to all US citizens.

After the Civil War (1861–1865), which resulted in abolishing the enslavement of Black people in the United States, the Fifteenth Amendment passed in 1870. This prohibited federal or state governments from denying the right to vote based on race. The amendment secured voting rights for Black men.

In the decades following the Seneca Falls Convention in 1848, women marched and protested for the right to vote. Susan B. Anthony, a leader in the women's suffrage movement, traveled around the country giving speeches and was arrested in 1872 for illegally voting. In 1917, another leader, Alice Paul, picketed for months outside the White House with more than 1,000 supporters, asking

Alice Paul led the National Woman's Party, which held demonstrations for women's right to vote in the years leading up to the Nineteenth Amendment.

for the right to vote. Her work helped get the Nineteenth Amendment passed in 1920, giving women the right to vote.

In the 1960s, the government drafted large numbers of young men 18 years old and older to fight in the Vietnam War (1954–1975). At that time, the voting age was 21. Young people protested that if they were old enough to fight in a war then they were old enough to vote. The Twenty-Sixth Amendment, ratified in 1971, expanded the voting age to citizens 18 years old and older.

THE VOTING RIGHTS ACT

Black Americans were disenfranchised long after the passage of the Fifteenth Amendment because of state laws. In 1964, the government ratified the Twenty-Fourth Amendment, which outlawed charging poll taxes or any other tax that could suppress people's right to vote in federal elections. The same year, Congress passed the Civil Rights Act of 1964, which banned segregation in public places and banned employment discrimination based on race, gender, religion, or nationality. Still, some state laws—such as the Jim Crow laws in the South—that kept Black Americans from voting continued to be passed and enforced.

The Voting Rights Act of 1965 struck down many of these laws on the grounds that they did not provide equal protection under the law. For example, the Voting Rights Act banned literacy tests for voters. These tests mainly targeted Black voters who tended to have higher rates of illiteracy than white voters due to lack of educational opportunities. Additionally, election officials scored the tests and could decide who passed or failed.

The Voting Rights Act also required the US Department of Justice to oversee the registration of voters in states where less than half of Black Americans who were eligible to vote were not registered. This federal oversight aimed

to ensure that states were not making voter registration unfair for Black citizens. The Voting Rights Act also required places with a history of discriminatory laws to have changes in their voting policies approved by the Department of Justice. The Voting Rights Act became a powerful tool for the federal government to enforce equal opportunities for all citizens to vote.

> "THROWING OUT [OVERSIGHT OF STATE VOTING LAWS] WHEN IT HAS WORKED AND IS CONTINUING TO WORK . . . IS LIKE THROWING AWAY YOUR UMBRELLA IN A RAINSTORM BECAUSE YOU ARE NOT GETTING WET."[7]
>
> —SUPREME COURT JUSTICE RUTH BADER GINSBURG, WHO DISAGREED WITH THE *SHELBY COUNTY V. HOLDER* RULING

In 2013, the US Supreme Court ruled in the landmark case of *Shelby County v. Holder* that the federal government's oversight of state voting laws should end. The majority of the court argued that the data that justified this oversight in 1965 was no longer applicable to conditions in 2013. Critics of this decision argued that it opened the door for many states to pass laws to once again suppress voting for certain groups of people.

As part of the civil rights movement, many people protested against Jim Crow laws, which separated people by race and prevented some Black Americans from voting.

MODERN VOTING
ISSUES

F ive US presidents received fewer individual votes than their opponent but still won their election. In the 2016 election, Democrat Hillary Clinton lost to Republican Donald Trump but received 2.9 million more votes.[1] The reason for this was the electoral college. It is one of a few parts of today's voting system that some people have criticized as being unfair or outdated. Some believe members of powerful political parties can unfairly manipulate parts of the voting system in their favor.

Today's elections are dominated by two political parties. Republicans, generally represented by the color red, are more politically conservative. The Republican Party platform, a document outlining

Hillary Clinton, *right*, and Donald Trump, *left*, participated in televised debates ahead of the 2016 election.

its stance on important issues, supports lower taxes, individual rights, military spending, and fewer government regulations. It also opposes abortion. Democrats, generally represented by the color blue, are more politically liberal. The Democratic Party platform supports government protection of workers, regulations to support consumers and the environment, higher tax rates for the wealthy, universal health care, and abortion access.

LOSING THE POPULAR VOTE

Before President Trump, four other presidents won the election without winning the popular vote. In 1824, John Quincy Adams lost both the popular vote and the electoral college vote. Andrew Jackson received the most votes in both cases. However, because there were more than two candidates, Jackson did not receive the 131 votes required to win a majority in the electoral college. The choice went to the House of Representatives, which voted to make Adams president. In 1876, President Rutherford B. Hayes lost the popular vote by a quarter of a million votes. He won the electoral college by one vote and became president. In 1888, President Benjamin Harrison lost the popular vote by 90,000 votes but won the electoral vote. In 2000, Al Gore won the popular vote by 540,000 but lost the election to President George W. Bush.[2]

ELECTORAL COLLEGE ISSUES

One of the reasons the writers of the US Constitution created the electoral college was to provide a buffer between the citizens and the presidential vote. Partly informed by their experiences with Great Britain's monarchy system, the

Founding Fathers feared that a tyrant might unduly influence the uneducated masses of people. They felt an educated electoral college would make a wiser choice.

Another reason for the electoral college was to protect states with smaller populations. More than half of the US population lives in just nine states. Under a popular vote, these states together could dominate presidential elections. The electoral college gives less-populous states the power to prevent that sort of situation by guaranteeing that each state has at least three of the 538 electoral votes cast for president. The rest of the votes are divided among states with more population. This distribution of electoral

BERNIE SANDERS: DEMOCRAT AND INDEPENDENT

In February 2019, Senator Bernie Sanders of Vermont filed with the Federal Election Commission to run as a Democrat in the US presidential race of 2020. A few weeks later, in March, he filed as an Independent to be reelected to the Senate in 2024. Sanders, who had long been an Independent senator, chose to run as a Democrat because it would be nearly impossible to win a presidential election as an Independent. This concerned many Democrats, as it had when Sanders did the same thing in the 2016 presidential election. As a result, the Democratic Party changed the rules for 2020. Anyone running to be the Democratic nominee must sign a pledge to serve as a Democratic president if elected. Sanders, whose policies have often been to the left of many Democratic ones, served 16 years in the House and was elected to his third term as an Independent in the Senate in 2018. He typically votes with the Democrats and has been accepted into positions of Democratic leadership in the Senate.

votes forces candidates to appeal to more parts of the country. States in different parts of the country may face different issues.

However, critics of the electoral college say this rule unfairly gives residents in states with small populations more power in national elections compared with people living in more populous states. For example, Wyoming has three electors, each representing 189,008 people in the state, while California has 55 electors, each representing 726,100 people.[3]

GERRYMANDERING

Another part of the voting system that has been scrutinized is the way that congressional districts are drawn. After the US Census every ten years, state legislatures create new voting

WHERE DID GERRYMANDERING GET ITS NAME?

The term *gerrymandering* comes from the name of Elbridge Gerry, a Massachusetts governor in the 1800s. Gerry managed to draw district lines that favored his Democratic Party over the Federalist Party even though the Federalists had won two-thirds of the vote. The resulting odd-shaped districts led a painter, Gilbert Stuart, to draw the strange district shape into a salamander. Benjamin Russell, editor of the *Boston Sentinel* newspaper, coined the term *gerrymander* (a combination of *Gerry* and *salamander*). Modern gerrymandered districts are often given names that represent their strange shapes, such as Ohio's "Lake Erie Monster" and Pennsylvania's "Goofy Kicking Donald Duck."[4]

districts within their states. Each district chooses its own representative. According to a 1964 US Supreme Court ruling, each district must have approximately the same number of people. But how the legislature draws the district lines can vastly influence whether a district votes primarily for Republicans or Democrats. Districts that will likely favor Republicans are called red districts, and those favoring Democrats are blue districts.

RED, BLUE, AND PURPLE

Most states that tend to vote Republican in presidential elections, called red states, are in the southern and central regions of the country. Most states that tend to vote Democratic in presidential elections, called blue states, are along the northeast and west coasts. Purple states, also called swing states or battleground states, are states that may swing toward either party.

Members of the ruling party in the legislature often draw the district lines to benefit their own party, a process called gerrymandering. Legislators may draw districts in a way that splits voters of the opposing party, maintaining a majority of their own voters in key districts. Or sometimes the ruling party's legislators put many of the opposing party's voters in one district so the ruling party can win all other districts. Another tactic is to add a population that

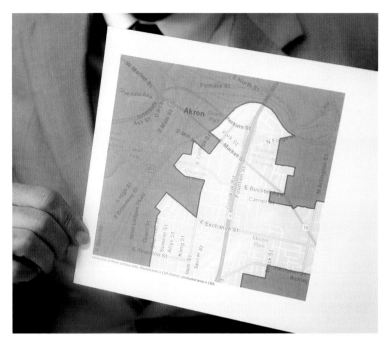

Gerrymandering leads to oddly shaped voting districts, such as this one in Ohio shown in 2019.

is likely to vote against an incumbent, such as a college campus, to a region where it will be the political minority.

Democratic and Republican legislators both practice gerrymandering to keep their own parties in power. For example, in the 2018 election for North Carolina's state legislature, Democrats received 50 percent of the votes for state Senate but got only 42 percent of the seats because of how seats are divided by district. The Democrats received 50.5 percent of the votes for state House but got only 45 percent of the seats.[5] The representation was disproportionate as a result of gerrymandering by the Republicans in power.

Gerrymandering can be harmful in several ways. It is often used to disenfranchise certain racial, cultural, or socioeconomic groups. Also, when legislatures use gerrymandering to create districts where incumbents don't have to face serious challenges during elections, members of Congress from these districts are less likely to compromise with the other party. This refusal to compromise, along with general differences in opinions, can contribute to a Congress that is slow to pass laws.

"I THINK WE'VE GOT TO END THE PRACTICE OF DRAWING OUR CONGRESSIONAL DISTRICTS SO THAT POLITICIANS CAN PICK THEIR VOTERS, AND NOT THE OTHER WAY AROUND."[7]

—PRESIDENT BARACK OBAMA, 2016

PRIMARIES AND CAUCUSES

Political parties choose their candidates for office in primaries or caucuses. In 2016, a Pew Research Center poll showed that only 35 percent of voters thought the system for nominating candidates to run for presidential office was effective.[6] Most states hold primary elections for people to vote for a candidate. States that hold closed primaries only allow people who are members of a party to vote for a presidential nominee of that party. States with open primaries allow everyone to vote for nominees of the parties.

Some states hold caucuses instead of primaries to choose presidential nominees. At a caucus, members of

Joe Biden, who eventually became the Democratic nominee for the 2020 election, was one of many candidates who started campaigning early in Iowa, the state with the first caucuses.

a party meet locally to discuss their choices before they vote. This can greatly restrict the number of people who participate because many voters may not be able to easily attend a long meeting to nominate a candidate. Compared with caucuses, voting in primaries is generally quicker. In addition, those who do attend caucuses often represent more passionate members of the party who follow politics closely, so the nominee may not reflect feelings of most voters in the party.

States don't all hold their caucuses and primaries on the same day. These voting events are staggered over months, generally from February to July of an election year. Some people believe that the process lasts too long and that too much power is given to states that vote early. Potential candidates must start campaigning and fundraising for more than a year before the election.

In 1972, the Republicans and Democrats agreed that Iowa, a caucus state, would hold the first vote of the year, followed by the New Hampshire primary. Since 1920, New Hampshire had always held the first primary vote. Iowa has a state law that says its caucuses are to be the first in the nation, and New Hampshire has a similar law declaring its

MORE TO THE
STORY

THE 2020
IOWA CAUCUSES

Many people have questioned whether Iowa and New Hampshire should be the first states to vote for presidential nominees. Neither is racially or economically representative of the country. They are both about 90 percent white, compared with approximately 60 percent of the country as a whole.[8] Additionally, some people say the caucus system used in Iowa is confusing, as it includes more than one round of voting with people changing their votes along the way. The caucuses can also take hours, which may make it difficult for some people to participate.

The 2020 Iowa Caucuses to select a Democratic nominee were widely considered a disaster. The Iowa Democratic Party chose an untested smartphone app to report votes. For the first time, the party required reporting of how votes were cast during the numerous votes in each caucus, slowing reporting from many caucuses. Backup phone lines jammed as caucus chairs tried to call in results. In the end, the Democrats had to count the backup paper ballots to certify the results, so Iowa's results were delayed for more than a week as other states' primary elections continued. It was a close race. In the end, Pete Buttigieg was declared the winner of the caucuses.

primary election as the first. Candidates spend months in these states meeting with voters. Media coverage is heavy. Candidates tailor their campaigns to meet the expectations of Iowa voters. A 2011 study by economists Brian Knight and Nathan Schiff concluded that a voter in these two states had five times the impact of a voter in other states.

Candidates tend to focus more campaigning on states that vote early because success in these states gives candidates momentum. It brings them more national attention and typically increases their fundraising. In 2020, Democratic candidate Joe Biden did not do well in Iowa or New Hampshire, but he rocketed to the front of the race by winning the third primary in South Carolina. He eventually became the Democratic Party's nominee that year.

DELEGATES

As in the electoral college, primary and caucus voters do not vote directly for their candidates. Party members elect representatives, called pledged delegates, to go to the national party convention to officially nominate their candidate. At the convention, the candidate is usually

President Trump accepts the Republican Party's nomination in 2016. Both parties officially select their presidential candidates at national conventions.

decided by the first vote. However, if one candidate does not receive enough votes to win the nomination, the delegates hold discussions until a candidate receives a majority vote.

In the 1970s, the Republican and Democratic parties began reforms to change the nomination process. Democrats expanded the number of delegates from each state to include more women and people of racial or cultural minorities in the nominating process.

Democrats also switched from a winner-take-all system to one that divided the delegates among candidates who receive more than 15 percent of the vote. In addition, Democrats added superdelegates in the 1980s. They make up about 15 percent of all delegates. The state party leaders select these delegates to give the party leadership more influence if the vote is close. In the Democratic Party, the superdelegates are not included in the first vote. They only vote if a second vote is required. Many people do not like the idea of the party leaders stepping in to make the final decision.

The Republican Party has fewer delegates. The only superdelegates are the three members of each state's national committee. If a second round of voting is required, any delegate can change his or her vote. Republicans in some states use a winner-take-all system so that all the delegates from the state will vote for the candidate who won the most votes. Other states use apportionment so that delegates vote for candidates according to the percentage of votes they received. In a winner-take-all situation, many voters have little chance of seeing their favorite candidate elected.

FROM THE HEADLINES

THIRD PARTIES

Third parties are official political parties outside of the big two, the Democratic Party and the Republican Party. As of September 2019, there were 224 third parties, although many were only recognized in one state.[9] Multistate parties include the Libertarian, Green, and Constitution Parties. Third parties have difficulty electing their candidates due to the high cost of running for office, lack of media attention, and federal campaign finance rules that require a lot of paperwork. But third parties often have influence by bringing attention to particular issues.

The Socialist Party made women's suffrage an issue in the late 1800s and early 1900s. Working with the Populist Party, this third party also brought attention to labor laws and succeeded in getting child labor laws passed and standardizing a 40-hour work week. The Reform Party, which nominated Ross Perot for president in 1992, got 19 percent of the popular vote and made budget deficits an important issue.[10]

Third parties are often considered spoilers in elections, drawing votes from one side or the other. In 2000, George W. Bush won the presidential election by 537 votes in Florida. Ralph Nader, running as a Green Party candidate that year, received 97,488 votes in Florida.[11] According to a *Political Science Quarterly* review, when Green voters were asked which candidate they would choose from only two candidates—Bush or his Democratic opponent, former Vice President Al Gore—they overwhelmingly supported Gore. Their votes would have been more than enough to win the election.

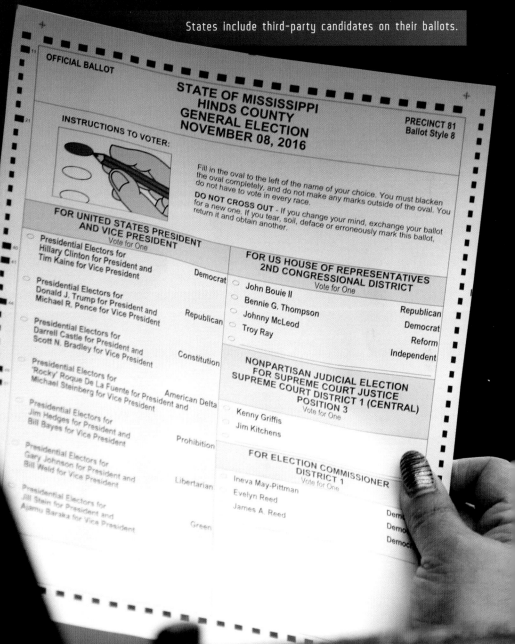

States include third-party candidates on their ballots.

OFFICIAL BALLOT

STATE OF MISSISSIPPI
HINDS COUNTY
GENERAL ELECTION
NOVEMBER 08, 2016

PRECINCT 81
Ballot Style 8

INSTRUCTIONS TO VOTER:

Fill in the oval to the left of the name of your choice. You must blacken the oval completely, and do not make any marks outside of the oval. You do not have to vote in every race.

DO NOT CROSS OUT - If you change your mind, exchange your ballot for a new one. If you tear, soil, deface or erroneously mark this ballot, return it and obtain another.

FOR UNITED STATES PRESIDENT
AND VICE PRESIDENT
Vote for One

Presidential Electors for
Hillary Clinton for President and
Tim Kaine for Vice President
Democrat

Presidential Electors for
Donald J. Trump for President and
Michael R. Pence for Vice President
Republican

Presidential Electors for
Darrell Castle for President and
Scott N. Bradley for Vice President
Constitution

Presidential Electors for
'Rocky' Roque De La Fuente for President and
Michael Steinberg for Vice President
American Delta

Presidential Electors for
Jim Hedges for President and
Bill Bayes for Vice President
Prohibition

Presidential Electors for
Gary Johnson for President and
Bill Weld for Vice President
Libertarian

Presidential Electors for
Jill Stein for President and
Ajamu Baraka for Vice President
Green

FOR US HOUSE OF REPRESENTATIVES
2ND CONGRESSIONAL DISTRICT
Vote for One

John Bouie II

Bennie G. Thompson
Republican

Johnny McLeod
Democrat

Troy Ray
Reform

Independent

NONPARTISAN JUDICIAL ELECTION
FOR SUPREME COURT JUSTICE
SUPREME COURT DISTRICT 1 (CENTRAL)
POSITION 3
Vote for One

Kenny Griffis

Jim Kitchens

FOR ELECTION COMMISSIONER
DISTRICT 1
Vote for One

Ineva May-Pittman

Evelyn Reed

James A. Reed

Dem

Demo

Democ

REFORMS

There are many proposed solutions to address the issues in today's voting system. Some people want to move away from the electoral college to choose a president by popular vote. People have also proposed ways to stop gerrymandering and to change the presidential nominating process. These proposed changes are heavily debated by politicians and members of the public.

A 2020 poll showed that 58 percent of American adults believed the Constitution should be amended to remove the electoral college. Forty percent wanted to keep it.[1] Democrats favor changing the electoral college more than Republicans do.

Some people believe voting in the electoral college would be fairer if states changed the way they choose their electors. The winner-take-all model of choosing

The 2016 election motivated some people to hold demonstrations related to the electoral college vote.

42

electors—used by 48 states and Washington, DC— means that a candidate only has to win 50.1 percent of the popular vote to get all of a state's electoral votes.[2] A candidate who wins 49.9 percent receives no electoral votes, so that candidate's many supporters get no voice.

The reason more states do not split electors is often that politicians want to maintain their party's power. For example, a state with three electors that historically always votes for one party may see 33 percent of its popular vote go to the other party. In that case, politicians in power for the majority party would not want to divide the electors, because that would give one elector to the minority party. Under the winner-takes-all system, the majority party would still get all of the electors.

PARTISANSHIP

Partisanship is loyalty to a political party. A 2019 Pew Research Center survey showed that members of both parties, 85 percent of Republicans and 78 percent of Democrats, feel that partisanship is getting worse, creating a deep divide that goes beyond political issues.[3] Most Republican survey participants saw Democrats as closed-minded, unpatriotic, and immoral. Most Democrats viewed Republicans as closed-minded, and almost half saw Republicans as immoral. In Congress, extreme partisanship can lead to lack of compromise between parties, resulting in little or no legislation passed.

PREVENTING GERRYMANDERING

Many people have expressed a desire to make voting district lines more fair. In all but four states, either the state legislators or committees of legislators, advisers, and elected officials are responsible for drawing congressional district boundaries. One way to prevent gerrymandering is to have independent commissions draw new districts. However, most states do not use independent commissions.

Some people propose not having district lines. Voters could vote for a party and then have the parties select representatives according to the proportion of votes they receive. Representatives would represent an entire state rather than a district, as senators do. If each party received 50 percent of the vote, each party would appoint half of the representatives. However, some people say this idea gives parties too much power. People also argue that representatives can get to know their constituents better if they are just working for a district rather than the whole state.

REFORMING THE NOMINATING PROCESS

Although parties have tried to make the process for nominating presidential candidates fair, there are many issues. Money plays a major role in candidates getting their names recognized. Those who don't have money for lots of advertisements and to travel all over the country often drop out of the process after only a few states vote.

One proposed solution for this problem is to have party leaders vet and select two candidates to go on the primary ballot. Then voters could decide. This would do away with unqualified candidates and plurality winners, which are candidates who win despite having less than 50 percent of support among voters. This can happen when top-tier candidates have similar platforms. For example, two candidates proposing free college tuition might run against a lone candidate on the other side. The majority of voters may support free college, but the two free-college candidates split their vote, so the issue is decided by the minority voting against the issue. Critics of parties vetting and selecting their candidates say that process would give party leaders too much power.

Presidential candidates and their supporters spend a lot of money and effort advertising their campaigns.

Political parties could also make the nominating process shorter. Primaries could run only a few months before the convention. This would make running for office less expensive because there would be fewer months of campaigning. People have also suggested rotating the order of primaries between the states or groups of states, rather than always having Iowa and New Hampshire vote first, so that no one state gets more leverage in choosing candidates.

Large-scale changes like those suggested are difficult to implement, partly because they are debated by members of both parties and Independents. Still, states have made smaller changes to solve voting issues. For example, states with open primaries allow everyone, including those not in a party, to vote for presidential nominees. And many states have chosen to hold primaries instead of caucuses, partly to make it easier for more people to participate. In 2020, only Iowa, Kentucky, Nevada, North Dakota, and Wyoming held caucuses to select presidential nominees. In addition, three territories, American Samoa, Guam, and the US Virgin Islands, held caucuses. Considering the issues surrounding the lack of representation among voters in these states and territories, many are considering moving to primaries.

INDEPENDENTS

Republicans and Democrats have dominated US politics for more than a century. But in 2020, approximately 34 percent of registered voters were Independents.[4] They are the fastest-growing segment of voters. The rise of Independents has followed a growing partisan divide in US politics as Democrats have become more liberal and Republicans have become more conservative. Many people with more moderate views feel pushed out of either party.

"(CAUCUSES ARE) LIKE A STUDENT BODY ELECTION. YOU HAVE TO RESPECT THE ABSURDITY OF IT OR IT'LL DRIVE YOU CRAZY."[5]

—STUART STEVENS, STRATEGIST FOR 2012 REPUBLICAN PRESIDENTIAL CANDIDATE MITT ROMNEY

A poll from May 2019 found that about 13 percent of Independents lean Republican and 17 percent lean Democratic.[6] This means they more often agree with that party's stance on issues and vote for that party's candidates. On some issues, especially social issues, Independents part from their leaning party. For example, 59 percent of Republican-leaning Independents favored allowing gays and lesbians to marry compared with 37 percent of Republicans.[7]

Independent voters who do not lean in either direction, known as swing voters, are often important in a close election. Most Democratic or Republican candidates can win voters in their own party. Candidates may put more effort campaigning in states with a lot of swing voters, giving these Independents an increasing amount of power.

THE RISE OF POLITICAL PARTIES

The US Constitution does not provide a means for nominating candidates to run for president. However, the process of nominating candidates using political parties, or groups of like-minded people, arose before 1800. At first, members of the party in Congress chose the nominee. Later, elite members of the party at state and local levels met to nominate a candidate. The system was very corrupt, with political party bosses often bribed with political favors or money to support particular candidates.

BARRIERS
TO VOTING

A 2018 Pew Research poll found that 67 percent of American voters thought everything possible should be done to make it easy for people to vote.[1] There was serious disagreement between the major parties about this issue. Eighty-four percent of Democratic voters agreed compared to only 48 percent of Republicans. Fifty-one percent of Republican voters said citizens should have to prove they want to vote by registering early.[2]

Some people argue that making voting difficult can be a way to keep members of opposing parties from voting. This tactic is called voter suppression. Since the end of federal oversight on state voting laws, many

One barrier to voting is when people have to wait in line for a long time.

NATIVE AMERICANS IN NORTH DAKOTA

In November 2018, the US Supreme Court upheld a new North Dakota law passed by a Republican legislature that required all voters to have an ID with a residential address when they voted at a polling place. As a result, an estimated 5,000 Native American voters, who tend to mostly vote Democratic, could not vote.[5] Many of the Native Americans living on reservations in North Dakota do not use street addresses; instead they use PO Box addresses. People without street addresses cannot get a state-issued ID card, and tribal identification cards without street addresses were not accepted as valid voter IDs under the new law. Lawsuits filed in 2019 forced the state government to work with tribal leaders to make sure Native Americans can access legal voting ID cards.

states have passed new laws making it more difficult for some people to vote.

One example is voter ID laws. Traditionally, many states have required a signature at a polling site to vote. In early 2020, 35 states required people to show identification to vote.[3] About half of these required a photo ID. Others accepted other forms of identification, such as a bank statement. Many voter ID laws disproportionately affect people of color, young people, people with disabilities, or people in rural areas. Only 8 percent of white people do not have a government-issued photo ID, compared with 25 percent of Black people.[4] Critics argue that the fact that some forms of ID are accepted while others aren't is a form of discrimination. For example, Texas accepts concealed weapons permits as IDs, but it does not accept student ID cards. People with low incomes often cannot afford a state voter ID card. Although the ID card is free, getting copies of the documents needed to apply for it, such as a birth certificate, costs money. Also, traveling to apply for a card is difficult for many rural or disabled citizens.

Republican state legislatures have been more likely to pass new voter ID laws. Supporters of these laws often say they are seeking to prevent voter fraud by tightening ID requirements. Opponents of voter ID laws point out that there have only been 31 cases of voter fraud, most of which were mistakes by a voter or poll worker, out of the approximately one billion votes made since 2000.[6] Voter ID laws in Texas and North Carolina have been overturned after being challenged in federal court. One federal appeals court found that North Carolina's law that required photo IDs at polls and restricted early voting targeted "African Americans with almost surgical precision."[7]

"I DON'T THINK [A VOTER ID REQUIREMENT] IS DISENFRANCHISEMENT. I THINK THAT AFRICAN AMERICANS THAT ARE CITIZENS OF [THE] UNITED STATES OF AMERICA CAN GET OUT AND VOTE."[8]

—REPRESENTATIVE ALLEN WEST OF FLORIDA, REPUBLICAN, 2012

LONG LINES AND LONG DISTANCE

Even if a person is registered to vote and has an acceptable ID, voting can be difficult. States determine how many polling places are in a community, when the polls are open, and whether citizens can vote early or by mail-in ballot.

The time it takes to vote can be a major problem for many people. When an area has few polling places, lines to vote may be longer. This may discourage people from voting. These are often people who have to go to work. Some states require employers to allow employees time off to vote, but this time off is sometimes unpaid or limited. Some people struggle to find time to vote because they must be at home to care for their children or others in their households.

In some cases, decisions about polling locations can make it difficult to even reach a polling site. In 2018, Dodge City, Kansas, moved the one polling place for 13,000 voters outside of the city. Instead of going to the local center, voters had to travel nearly 3 miles (4.8 km) out of town to a location where there was no bus service.[9]

States in the South that were once under federal oversight have closed 1,200 polling places since 2013. Seven counties in Georgia have only one polling place each. Texas has closed 10 percent of voting sites, and Arizona has closed 20 percent.[10]

Not having a nearby polling location means people must take more time to vote, often having to leave work or make arrangements for child care.

In Wisconsin, the Republican-led state legislature decided not to postpone its 2020 primary election during the COVID-19 pandemic. Health experts worldwide were recommending that people avoid gathering in crowds in order to avoid spreading the new viral disease COVID-19, which had no vaccine and no cure. Wisconsin governor Tony Evers tried to delay the election amid the concerns about COVID-19,

WAITING TO VOTE

In the 2020 Texas primary, Hervis Rogers stood for more than six hours in line, finally casting his vote after 1:30 a.m. before going to work on the night shift.[11] Many others in line gave up and left. Officials knew that Democratic turnout in the heavily contested primary would be much higher than in the almost uncontested Republican primary. President Trump was expected to easily take the Republican nomination, but the race to decide who would be his Democratic opponent was competitive. Texas officials had assigned the same number of voting machines to each party. Democrats waited for hours to vote while Republican machines sat idle.

but he was overruled. Those who supported continuing with the primary election as planned cited an interest in protecting the integrity of elections. The decision was criticized by some members of both political parties across the country. In Milwaukee, a city of 600,000, there were five polling sites open compared with the previous 180.[12] Part of the reason Milwaukee officials chose to have fewer polling places was to help people stay safely distanced from one another during the pandemic. People stood in line for hours, many in the rain, to vote. In addition to the presidential primary, local issues were on the ballot, including the high-profile reelection bid of a conservative state supreme

US TERRITORIES AND VOTING

People who live in some territories of the United States, such as Puerto Rico, the US Virgin Islands, and Guam, are US citizens but cannot vote for president. Citizens of the territories can vote in primary elections to nominate candidates for president and vice president because the primaries are held by the political parties and not the government. But they cannot vote in presidential elections because the US Constitution mandates that the president is elected by states, not territories. Each territory is entitled to one representative in Congress, but those representatives cannot vote; they can only speak on issues. As US citizens, people who live in Puerto Rico may freely move to any state, establish residency in the state, and vote. On the other hand, if someone moves from a state to live in Puerto Rico, the person loses his or her vote. The territories include approximately 3.4 million US citizens. These people can serve in the military and receive federal benefits, but they cannot vote for president.

court justice, who ended up losing his seat to a more

liberal candidate.

MAIL-IN AND EARLY VOTING

State government leaders make the laws regarding

options for mail-in and early voting. Some states allow

people to request a mail-in ballot instead of going to the

polls. Others require those voting with a mail-in ballot to

have an excuse, such as being out of state on Election Day.

New Jersey was one of the states to expand mail-in voting
options during the COVID-19 pandemic.

ONLINE VOTING

Many states let people register to vote online and apply for an absentee ballot online. In 2019, 20 states allowed voting online, but only for some voters.[14] For example, Utah allows people with disabilities to return ballots online. Many states were considering adding or expanding online voting options during the COVID-19 pandemic. However, officials worried about the potential for hacking if the majority of voting was conducted online.

The most common use of online ballots is for military members serving overseas. The Uniformed and Overseas Citizens Absentee Voting Act requires states to allow military members to vote using an absentee ballot. Some states fulfill this requirement by using a secured internet connection.

During the COVID-19 pandemic, many states expanded their options for mail-in voting.

Five states—Colorado, Hawaii, Oregon, Washington, and Utah—conduct all of their voting by mail.[13] This means that every registered voter is mailed a ballot. Many voters like the system because they can take time to look over the issues on the ballot, and it is generally considered convenient. States may save money by not having to staff polling places and buy voting machines. Voting by mail can increase voter turnout. People do not have to take off work or disrupt their schedules to vote. This was particularly evident during the 2020 primaries, when people were reluctant to go to polls due to the COVID-19 pandemic. For example, Montana saw a record turnout for its 2020 primary election, which was all conducted by mail due to the pandemic. The voter turnout was more than 55 percent, compared with 45 percent in 2016.[15]

There are disadvantages to mail-in voting. Some areas have poor postal service. Influence from family members or others is more likely when someone is casting a vote at home instead of alone in a voting booth. It takes an initial investment for states to go to all mail-in ballots, and election results are often slower. Some people, notably some Republican politicians, have said that voting by mail increases fraud and favors Democratic candidates. However, in a study at Stanford University, researchers found that mail-in voting gave no advantage to either Democrats or Republicans.

Increasing voter turnout can also be accomplished by increasing the length of time to vote. Nine states do not allow people to vote in person before Election Day. Other states allow early voting ranging from four to 45 days before an election. Weekend voting is allowed in more than half of the early voting states. This makes voting easier for people who work during the week and might have difficulty voting on Election Day.

CHAPTER SIX

LOSING THE
RIGHT TO VOTE

The right to vote is available to any citizen of the 50 states, but it is a right that can be taken away. One way someone may lose the right to vote is by being convicted of a crime. In early 2020, only one state, Iowa, banned anyone with a felony conviction from voting even after the person had served the prison time and paid the related fines.[1] But in August, the state's governor issued an executive order to expand voting rights for felons. Some states restore voting rights when a person is released from prison or finishes serving probation or parole. Other states wait until a certain amount of time has passed or make people apply individually to restore their right to vote. Two states, Vermont and Maine, allow all felons to vote.[2]

A woman fills out her voter registration form in 2019 after Florida restored voting rights for people with felony convictions.

"ONCE A PERSON HAS SERVED THEIR TIME, THEY SHOULD NOT BE MADE TO CONTINUE PAYING FOR THEIR PAST MISTAKES."[4]

—DESMOND MEADE, PRESIDENT OF THE FLORIDA RIGHTS RESTORATION COALITION

RACKING UP FEES

It is expensive for a person accused of a crime to go to court, even if the court ends up deciding the person is innocent. States charge a whole range of fees to move through the judicial system. In North Carolina, people are charged $60 to determine whether they are too poor to afford a lawyer—even though the right to an attorney is guaranteed by law. If accused people cannot afford bail, they are charged $10 a day while they are in jail waiting for their trial. If the prosecutor has to test evidence at the state crime lab, the person on trial must pay $600. And the fees don't end when a person is released from jail. People on probation or parole must pay $40 a month for supervision fees. If they are put on electronic monitoring, they are charged $90 a month. Other states have high numbers of similar fees too. In Ohio, there are 118 different fees.[5]

In 2019, almost six million people could not vote due to past felony convictions.[3] Felony convictions fall more heavily on low-income people and on people of color, especially Black and Hispanic people. This means that the votes of people in these groups are more likely affected by these laws.

The ability to vote is also affected by laws that require people to pay any court fees, fines, or restitution fees they owe before they can vote. This can be a substantial amount of money, and people who were already impoverished before their conviction often cannot pay. In 2019, approximately ten million people owed fines or fees of $50 billion as a result of criminal convictions.[6] In Alabama, 100,000 people had

been removed from the state's official voter list by 2017

because they owed the state

money. On average, they owed

about $5,000 each.[7]

REMOVING VOTERS FROM THE ROLLS

Federal laws require that

states maintain current voter

lists, called voting rolls. Maintaining these lists includes

removing people who have moved away or died. However,

federal law says states can remove people from their rolls

for not voting. Once people are removed from the voting

rolls, they have to register again in order to vote.

In 2018, the US Supreme Court ruled in an Ohio case

that voters could be removed from the voting rolls if

they did not vote for two years, did not return a notice

that they were being removed, and then did not vote for

another four years. Only 20 percent of people who were

sent notices returned them to update their addresses.[8]

This indicates that many people likely ignored such notices

FLORIDA FELONY VOTE

Florida had one of the strictest felony disenfranchisement laws in the country. Felons who had served their time were required to ask the governor of the state to restore their right to vote. Approximately 10 percent of Florida adults were disenfranchised due to felony convictions. In the Black population, this rose to more than 21 percent.[11] In November 2018, Florida passed a state constitutional amendment ending felony disenfranchisement for those who had completed their sentence, except for people convicted of murder or felony sex crimes. The number of potential voters in Florida, an important swing state in many presidential elections, increased by about 1.5 million.[12]

and were removed without their knowledge.

Activists often accuse states of attempting to purge the voting rolls, or remove voters not favorable to the party in power. In 2019, Wisconsin election officials sent notices to about 230,000 voters who they believed might have changed their home addresses.[10] The state planned to give voters until spring 2021 to respond, after the 2020 elections. A conservative group, the Wisconsin Institute for Law and Liberty, sued to have the voters removed from the voting rolls immediately. Liberal groups opposed this, believing that young people and poor people were more likely to be affected since they tend to move more often. The case went to court and a judge ordered the voters to be removed within 30 days. In February 2020, a Wisconsin appeals court overturned the ruling.

Activists protest outside the US Supreme Court building in 2018 as the court listens to arguments about whether voters should be allowed to be removed from the rolls.

COMPETENCE

US citizens in 39 states and in Washington, DC, can lose their right to vote due to a determination of mental incompetence.[13] This may range from new voters with autism or schizophrenia to older voters with dementia. There are no clear guidelines on when people are capable of voting and when they are not. The decision is often made by a judge during a hearing that provides a legal guardian for an individual. About 1.5 million adults in the United States have a guardian.[14]

These decisions for guardianship usually deal with someone taking care of another person's finances or health issues. Loss of the right to vote is usually a side issue. Still, judges in these guardianship hearings consider whether the person is capable of making a political decision. Some judges may strip the right to vote from someone who can't name the local mayor, even though some people without disabilities may not be able to name their mayor either.

Supporters of competency laws worry about fraud. A guardian may unduly influence someone's vote or even sway large numbers of people in a care facility to vote a particular way. This, however, would be fraud on the part of the caregiver, not the voter. Many argue that these voters should not lose their civil rights due to someone else's fraud.

Opponents of competency laws point out that some people with mental disabilities may be competent but simply have trouble communicating. This may be true of someone with autism who is very intelligent but struggles to maintain conversations with other people. Some states are revising their laws so that competency is more standardized. California, with 32,000 residents who have lost their right to vote due to mental incompetence, passed a new law in 2016 that gave the right to vote to anyone declared incompetent who expressed a desire to vote. Other states issued guidelines that say a person must understand the "nature and effect" of voting.[17] They should be able to answer questions about why they want to vote for a particular candidate. However, critics argue that this is a much tougher standard than most voters have to pass.

FIRST VOTE

Greg Demer has autism. He is very intelligent and has an interest in history and aviation. But he has trouble communicating. He doesn't know what to say when he meets someone new, so sometimes he just quotes from movies. As Demer got older, his mother worried about him making decisions regarding money or his health as an adult. So she went to court and was granted guardianship of her son when he turned 18 years old. The judge decided that if Demer couldn't make decisions about money then he couldn't make decisions about voting. But Demer was competent enough to work at a museum where he restored military aircraft. Tom Coleman, legal director of the Spectrum Institute, an organization that supports the rights of people with cognitive disabilities, did not think this was right. He went to court representing Demer, and a new judge restored Demer's voting rights. Ten years after Demer lost his vote, he was finally able to fill out a ballot.[18]

CHAPTER SEVEN

SECURITY AND SOCIAL MEDIA
ISSUES

E lection security is important to all voters. People want to know their votes are counted. They also want to make sure that votes are not cast illegally by people not eligible to vote. Attempts by Russia to influence the 2016 election and unfounded rumors of voting fraud shook many voters' confidence in the US election system. David Becker, founder of the nonprofit Center for Election and Innovation Research, says that about 40 percent of voters will question whether an election was fair if their candidate loses.[1]

After the 2016 presidential election, President Trump set up the Presidential Advisory Commission on Election

President Trump, *left*, stands with Kris Kobach, who helped lead Trump's Commission on Election Integrity in 2016.

Integrity to investigate, among other things, whether millions of undocumented immigrants voted in 2016. Republican Kris Kobach, the secretary of state of Kansas who served as vice chair of the commission, claimed the commission found more than 1,000 criminal convictions of voter fraud since 2000 and 8,400 instances of double voting in 2016.[2] However, sources for the information were never given, and the commission disbanded without presenting any evidence of illegal voting.

Some scholars doubted these claims by Kobach. They noted that even if 1,000 people had committed voter fraud, that is a very small number from the more than one billion votes that have been cast since 2000. In addition, double voting could be a case of a clerical error rather than intentional fraud by a voter. Experts conclude that there is no evidence that voter fraud is a big problem in the United States. Still, voter fraud is often used as a reason for more rigorous registration and ID laws as well as purging voter rolls. In 2018, Pew Research found that 57 percent of Republicans thought making it easier to vote makes elections less secure.[3]

Some voters must insert paper ballots into machines at their polling places. Other polling places have touch screen voting machines.

ELECTION SYSTEMS

Many people who are concerned about election security point to the integrity of the election systems as a serious issue. Most voters who cast their votes at polling places use voting machines. The machines are often decades old and outdated. They do not provide a way to audit or verify the vote. Many machines also do not provide a paper trail—a system to show on paper how votes were cast in case the machine fails. Officials worry that the inability to verify election results on paper will leave citizens questioning

HANGING CHADS

The 2000 presidential election between Republican George W. Bush and Democrat Al Gore was decided in Florida by 537 votes out of the six million that were cast.[4] One of the issues in Florida was that some voting machines did not completely punch through voting cards, resulting in hanging chads, or fragments of paper left by incomplete punches. Election officials were left examining the ballots by hand, often using a magnifying glass to determine a voter's intent. The results of the presidential election swung back and forth for weeks. In the end, the US Supreme Court decided the election by denying a recount of the ballots. It was the closest US presidential election in modern history.

election results. The perception that ballots were not counted fairly can result in people not trusting the democratic process.

States that want to update their voting machines face several obstacles. The first is money. Changing a voting system is expensive, and most states do not have the money in their budgets to cover the cost. In 2018, Congress granted $380 million to states for election security and an additional $425 million in 2019. The COVID-19 aid bill passed in March 2020 provided an additional $400 million for election security in anticipation of the 2020 presidential election. Still, some critics doubted this would be enough to protect the 2020 presidential election.

Another issue is time. Federal elections occur every two years. States need time to purchase equipment, verify that it works correctly, and then train poll workers and election officials on how to use the new technology.

Officials in many states that used paperless voting

machines only had a year and a

half to change systems between

the November 2018 elections

and the start of the presidential

primaries in February 2020.

HACKING

The US Department of

Homeland Security found that

21 states had their election

systems probed by Russian

hackers leading up to the 2016

elections.[5] A small number of

these hackers successfully got

into computers used by election

officials or campaigns. However,

US officials found no evidence

that votes were changed. In 2018, 45 percent of voters said

they were very or somewhat confident that elections are

safe from hacking.[6]

In 2020, 72 percent of Americans surveyed said they believed foreign governments would try to influence the presidential election again.[7] Cybersecurity experts say that paper ballots are essential to protecting the security of voting. Although voting machines are not always online, they are connected to voting systems that tabulate votes and share that data over the internet. Also, there are few people who can check to make sure that a machine has not been compromised when it arrives at a polling place or fix a technical glitch during an election. Because of the high cost of voting machines, states may close some polls because there are not enough machines available, resulting in long lines.

"THE INTELLIGENCE COMMUNITY HAS BEEN CLEAR THAT THE THREAT AND DESIRE TO UNDERMINE CONFIDENCE IN OUR DEMOCRATIC INSTITUTIONS REMAINS."[8]

—MATT MASTERSON, SENIOR CYBERSECURITY ADVISER IN THE DEPARTMENT OF HOMELAND SECURITY, 2018

Many people believe the United States should return to using paper ballots that can be scanned with optical scanners, which are like the devices used to scan bar codes, for counting. A 2018 National Academies of Sciences report cited this as the most secure method and said it costs less than new voting machines. This security gives people confidence that their votes will be counted correctly. "Voter confidence is a really big thing, and it's the battle I worry about losing," said Pennsylvania's elections commissioner, Jonathan Marks.[9]

SOCIAL MEDIA

Even with strong election security, many Americans worry about media and social media influence on elections. According to Pew Research, in 2019, 55 percent of adults said they "often" or "sometimes" got their news from social media—an 8 percentage point increase from 2018.[10] Slightly more than half of adults got news from Facebook.

Mainstream newspapers and television news programs may have biases, but their reporters are typically held responsible for the content reported. News reporters

CHANGING MEDIA

Newspapers were once the primary source of news, but in 2018, according to Pew Research, only 16 percent of Americans got their news from print newspapers. Most Americans, 44 percent, preferred to get news on television. Thirty-four percent preferred to get news online—up from 28 percent in 2016. In 2018, 20 percent of adults said they "often" got news on social media, with Facebook dominating the market, although of these, 57 percent said they thought the news on social media platforms was mostly inaccurate.[11]

can be fired for reporting mistruths. On social media, there typically are no consequences for lying. Some people believe that social media platforms should not be responsible for the content they display, even if that

People can't always be sure that what they read on social media is true.

content incites violence or is blatantly false. Others believe that as social media becomes a more influential source of news, the platforms should make an effort to ensure that they are not outlets for hate speech or misinformation.

Social media influence is a huge issue because of the high volume of information shared on these websites. Although computer algorithms may catch a lot of problematic content, it takes people to monitor and correct misinformation. Facebook learned this after it replaced 26 writers and editors with computer programs. This resulted in a fake story making it onto Facebook's Trending Topics section.

CHAPTER EIGHT

MONEY IN
ELECTIONS

I t takes money to run for office. Presidential candidates need funds to pay the people who manage the campaigns and run their state campaign offices. They need money for travel and lodging. They need a lot of money for advertising, including signs, radio and television ads, online marketing, and even campaign clothing. Campaigns also need employees to do the things every business needs, such as making budgets.

The cost of campaigning rises every year. Campaign spending by presidential candidates was four times as much in 2012 as in 2000.[1] In 2016, the top two candidates spent a combined total of $2.4 billion.[2]

Presidential candidates set up campaign offices across the country, such as Massachusetts senator Elizabeth Warren's Nevada office in 2020.

Then in the 2018 midterms, Congressional candidates spent about $5.7 billion total.[3] For candidates to win, they need to get their names and faces in front of voters.

Many people oppose the high cost of campaigning because it keeps the average person from running. Voters get less choice. Some voters say they want politicians to spend their time working on important issues instead of raising money. They want to see new rules about money in politics.

"DEMOCRACY IS ONE PERSON, ONE VOTE, AND A FULL DISCUSSION OF THE ISSUES THAT AFFECT US. OLIGARCHY IS BILLIONAIRES BUYING ELECTIONS, VOTER SUPPRESSION, AND A CONCENTRATED CORPORATE MEDIA DETERMINING WHAT WE SEE, HEAR AND READ."[4]

—SENATOR BERNIE SANDERS

CITIZENS UNITED

In 1974, Congress amended the Federal Election Campaign Act of 1971 to ensure that individuals did not sway elections by contributing large amounts of money to candidates. It also passed disclosure laws for federal candidates, political parties, and other political groups. Individuals are allowed to contribute up to $2,800 to a candidate. Congress created the Federal Election Commission (FEC) to oversee campaign finance laws.

These rules were challenged in 1975 in the US Supreme Court case *Buckley v. Valeo*. Opponents of the law argued that limiting political contributions violated the First Amendment right to free speech. In 1976, the US Supreme Court ruled that limiting political contributions to individual candidates did not violate the First Amendment and that it guarded the US system of democracy. However, the court also determined that candidates should not have limits on spending their own money to get elected. In addition, the court ruled there could be no restriction of political spending from groups outside the candidate or political party, and there could be no limit on total campaign expenditures.

In 2010, the US Supreme Court heard another case, *Citizens United v. Federal Election Commission*, that further

SMALL DONORS

Less than 10 percent of people ever donate to a candidate for political office. Money from small donors generally amounts to about 13 percent of money spent by a candidate.[5] In the 2020 Democratic primary, candidates emphasized the online contributions of small donors. Candidate Bernie Sanders raised $18.2 million in three months with 80 percent of the money raised coming from people contributing less than $200.[6] The success of online fundraising owes much success to microtargeting, or using data collected from numerous sources including social media to target advertising at individuals likely to donate. Some people are concerned about the lack of transparency in how corporations collect data on individuals and sell it to political campaigns.

opened elections to unlimited spending by outside groups. The case came about when Citizens United, a nonprofit group, wanted to spend money showing and advertising a film criticizing then senator Hillary Clinton as a presidential candidate just before the 2008 presidential primaries. The court ruled in favor of Citizens United, saying that corporations and other outside groups had no limitations on political spending. With this ruling, corporations could now spend as much as they wanted to help their preferred candidates, as long as the corporations did not directly coordinate with a candidate or political party.

PACs AND SUPER PACs

Political action committees (PACs) are organizations formed to support certain issues or candidates. They can donate money to a candidate, but there are limits to how much they can donate. PACs can only receive certain amounts from individuals and can only contribute $5,000 per year to a candidate.[7]

After the Citizens United case, new organizations called super PACs formed to raise unlimited money from

There are PACs and super PACs supporting politicians from both parties.

individuals and spend unlimited funds on campaigns.

The distinction between PACs and super PACs is that

super PACs cannot contribute to or work directly with a

candidate. Instead, they can spend unlimited money on

advertising as long as the ads are produced by the super

PAC independently. Although super PACs are required to

disclose their donors, individuals have found ways to avoid

exposure through dark money, or secret contributions.

One way to contribute dark money is to form nonprofit

organizations that in turn donate the money. Nonprofits

are not required to disclose donors.

The amount of money spent by super PACs has

become a huge issue in elections. Since money can be

hidden, wealthy donors and even foreign governments

have a way to sway elections in their favor. In the 2014

Senate races, at least 71 percent of outside spending for winning candidates came from dark money.[8] Critics say this undermines the democratic process and gives voters little confidence that their votes actually count. Proponents of unlimited spending by individuals or super PACs point out that people have a right to spend their money as they want. They feel the government is limiting their rights by limiting their direct financial support to candidates.

WHO DONATES THE MOST?

Between 2010 and 2020, 25 individuals or couples donated 47 percent of all money ($1.4 billion) given to super PACs. They represent both liberal and conservative views. Conservative donors Sheldon and Miriam Adelson gave the most money, at $292 million. The second-highest donor was businessman Tom Steyer with $255 million.[9] Steyer also ran for the Democratic presidential nomination in 2020 but eventually dropped out of the race. By July 15, 2020, 1,853 super PACs had formed and raised more than $883 million for the 2020 elections.[10] The largest Democratic super PAC is Priorities USA, which said it would spend $150 million in the 2020 presidential election to defeat President Trump.[11] The group said it would concentrate on spending for TV and digital advertising in four battleground states: Florida, Wisconsin, Michigan, and Pennsylvania.

DISCLOSURE AND PUBLIC FINANCING

There is a strong desire by voters to change the system that allows unlimited money to influence elections. An October 2017 poll by the *Washington Post* and the University of Maryland found that 94 percent of Americans believe that donations by the wealthy are responsible for much of the political dysfunction of the government.[12] In another poll by NBC News and the *Wall Street Journal*, 77 percent of registered voters said the single most important factor in their vote for Congress was getting rid of the influence of people or groups seeking to sway the government for their own benefit.[13] The only ways to overturn the *Citizens United* decision are a reversal by the US Supreme Court or an amendment to the Constitution. Neither of these are expected to happen quickly or easily.

One way to counter the influence of dark money in elections is to enforce disclosure laws. Congress could pass

Some people believe super PAC funding leads to corruption.

laws that would expose dark money. This would let voters make more informed decisions by knowing who is paying for advertising for or against a candidate. In addition, the FEC has not rigorously enforced laws regarding coordination between campaigns and super PACs.

Public financing of elections is another way to counter large dark money contributions. Congress approved public funding of elections in 1974. This means that governments can provide money to candidates who are running for election. As of 2020, less than one-half of the states had passed public financing laws.

There are two types of public financing programs offered by states: clean elections programs and

THE BILLIONAIRE INFLUENCE

With so much money needed to run a presidential campaign, billionaires have begun funding their own campaigns. In the 2020 election, two billionaires ran in the Democratic primaries: activist Tom Steyer and former New York City mayor Michael Bloomberg. The Republican candidate running for reelection, President Trump, was also a billionaire. People have wondered whether it's possible for billionaires to buy a US election. A January 2020 poll by the *Economist* magazine found that 10 percent of Americans said being a billionaire made a candidate more favorable, 29 percent less favorable, and 49 percent thought it made no difference.[14] Steyer dropped out of the 2020 primaries early, and, although Bloomberg spent $215 million on TV and radio ads in early primary states, he only won a few delegates before dropping out.[15] Bloomberg later pledged to spend up to $1 billion to defeat President Trump in 2020.

matching funding programs. Clean elections programs, which are offered in states such as Connecticut, Maine, and Arizona, offer full funding to candidates. In these programs, candidates are encouraged to collect small contributions—no more than five dollars—to prove they have public support, but they are not allowed to accept large private donations.[16] In matching funding programs, such as those in Hawaii and Florida, the state provides campaigns with partial election funding. Candidates can receive a portion of their funding from the state according to how much money they raise within limits set by the state.

In *Buckley v. Valeo*, the Supreme Court struck down a mandate of the FEC that required public financing for presidential elections. In addition, the court ruled that states cannot force candidates to use public financing. If candidates do choose to use public financing, they are not allowed to accept donations. The result is that most candidates do not use public financing, since the money is much less than what they can get with donations.

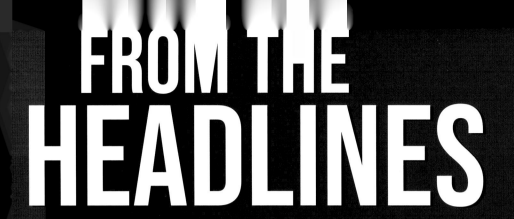

FROM THE HEADLINES

THE RISING COST OF PRESIDENTIAL ELECTIONS

The 2012 presidential race, which resulted in the reelection of Barack Obama, included the first billion-dollar campaigns in US history.

1992: George H. W. Bush, Bill Clinton, and Ross Perot spent $195.6 million combined.

2000: George W. Bush and Al Gore each spent about $200 million.

2004: George W. Bush spent $345 million for reelection.

2008: Barack Obama spent $730 million to beat John McCain.

2010: The ruling in *Citizens United v. FEC* allowed corporations and other groups to spend unlimited funds on elections.

2012: President Obama spent $722.4 million for reelection. The Democratic National Committee added $292.2 million. PAC spending was $131.7 million. This made for the first billion-dollar campaign at $1.14 billion with spending for both candidates equaling $2.6 billion.

2016: Donald Trump spent $440 million, $66 million from his own pocket, while Hillary Clinton spent $768.5 million. The combined total for both candidates, including PACs and party contributions, was $2.4 billion. This was the only election in modern history where the winning candidate spent less than his opponent.[17]

2020: Spending estimates for the 2020 elections were between $6 billion and $10 billion dollars just for political ads.[18]

ENCOURAGING PEOPLE TO VOTE

I n the 2016 presidential election, 27.3 percent of eligible voters voted for Donald Trump. Another 28.5 percent voted for Hillary Clinton, and 41.3 percent of eligible voters did not vote.[1] People who don't vote make a difference. Getting people registered to vote and to the polls is a major issue for candidates. Political campaigns understand that for candidates to be elected or for their policies to be enacted, they have to encourage people to get out and vote.

In seeking to increase voter turnout, US politicians like to look at voting blocs, or groups of people they believe vote the same way. Voting blocs might be

Colleges and other communities often hold events that encourage people to register to vote.

grouped according to gender, education level, ethnic group, socioeconomic group, age, or whether they live in urban or rural areas. Although everyone in a group does not necessarily vote the same way, people in these groups often have common interests. For example, young people might be more interested in the high cost of education while older people might be more concerned with protecting policies that benefit seniors.

For candidates running on particular issues, it is important to get voters who are interested in those issues to the polls. The problem for many candidates is that some voter groups are more likely to vote than others.

ELECTIONS WHERE ONE VOTE MADE THE DIFFERENCE

Many people don't vote because they think their one vote doesn't matter. However, there have been several times that one vote did matter. In 1910, Democrat Charles B. Smith took a New York congressional seat over the Republican incumbent, winning 20,685 to 20,684. In 1994, two candidates for Wyoming's House of Representatives tied. The governor broke the tie by drawing a ping-pong ball from a hat.[2]

Women vote at slightly higher rates than men. There are also more women in the United States than men.

Wealthy people tend to vote more than impoverished people. They are also more likely to be involved in the political process, from participating in protests to volunteering as campaign workers. Higher education also correlates with greater rates of voter participation.

People of color are less likely to vote than white people. This is often due to problems in voting systems, such as lack of access to polls. People of color are more than twice as likely than white people to have problems with voter IDs or registration. They are also more likely to be unable to vote due to illness, lack of transportation, or time constraints.

> "WE'VE GOT TO VOTE, VOTE, VOTE, VOTE. THAT'S IT; THAT'S THE WAY WE MOVE FORWARD."[3]
>
> —FORMER FIRST LADY MICHELLE OBAMA

YOUNG VOTERS

People in older generations vote more than those in younger generations. A study released in 2020 by the nonprofit Knight Foundation found that voters age 18 to 24 were less informed and less interested in politics than older voters, with 38 percent of them saying they didn't know enough to know who to vote for. Of all age groups, these young people were the least likely to vote in the 2020 presidential elections. The Knight Foundation report also showed that 26 percent of young voters didn't care about politics and 17 percent

didn't think their vote would matter.[4]

Young voters are also more likely to have time

constraints or to have moved recently than older people.

Stability plays an important role in the youth vote. If a

Former First Lady Michelle Obama has campaigned for When We All Vote, one of many organizations aimed at encouraging people to vote.

person moves a lot or changes jobs often, which many young people do, it is harder to register and to vote than if a person is a longtime resident homeowner. Registering to vote can mean doing the paperwork to change addresses, finding or purchasing the appropriate ID information, and getting to an unfamiliar polling place.

MAKING VOTING EASIER

A state's registration laws have a profound impact on who votes. In most states, people must register to vote before Election Day. Registration is often a process that takes time and effort that people may not be willing to put in—especially if registration is required weeks before an election. In a few states, people can register on Election Day. This makes

HISTORIC 2018 ELECTION

In the 2018 midterm elections, voters turned out in record numbers among every age bracket and racial group. According to the US Census, approximately 53 percent of all citizens of voting age cast a ballot, an 11 percentage point increase in voter turnout from that of 2014. It was the highest midterm turnout in 40 years. Forty percent of voters used alternative voting, such as early voting or mail-in voting. Among racial groups, the Asian vote and Hispanic vote each increased by 13 percentage points. Black voters increased by approximately 11 percentage points, and white voters increased by approximately 12 percentage points. Among those 18 to 29 years old, turnout went from 20 percent in 2014 to 36 percent in 2018—the largest percentage point increase for any group. The election results were significant. The House of Representatives swung from Republican to Democratic control.[5]

WORLDWIDE COMPULSORY VOTING

About 13 percent of all countries in the world require citizens to vote.[7] In some of these countries, there is no penalty imposed for not voting, or the law is basically ignored. In other countries penalties for not voting range from fines to losing the right to vote to losing social services. In some countries, a citizen can be jailed for not voting, although there are no documented cases of this happening. Those in favor of compulsory voting believe that having all citizens vote makes the government more representative. It also keeps campaigns from having to target nonvoters, thus saving time and money. Those opposed to compulsory voting argue that people should have the freedom to decide whether to vote. Compulsory voting may also encourage so-called "throw away votes," or people just randomly marking the ballot to fulfill their duty. Countries with compulsory voting tend to have about a 7 percent higher turnout than those without it.[8] Only 20 percent of Americans favor compulsory voting in the United States, according to a Pew Research poll.[9]

registration easier, since voters don't have to remember to register early for an election.

People who want to make it easy to register to vote propose making registration automatic when citizens first interact with the state, such as when they apply for a driver's license. As of October 2019, 16 states and Washington, DC, had automatic registration, and many more states had legislation pending. Automatic registration increases the number of people on the voting rolls.[6]

Automatic registration doesn't always translate to citizens actually voting. Some people aren't aware or don't remember that they are registered. Washington, DC, has addressed this issue by sending a reminder postcard to registered voters before an election. The result is a greater percentage of automatically registered voters actually voting compared with self-registered voters.

Even for those registered, casting a ballot takes time. Some people have proposed making Election Day a national holiday. Employers would give workers the day off, making it easier to vote. Making registration and voting easier especially impacts young voters who are new to the process. In a 2020 report by the Knight Foundation,

As voting issues continue to be discussed, many people hope voting and voter registration will become easier.

15 percent of nonvoters ages 18 to 24 claimed they would

be motivated to vote if they could vote online.[10]

Voting issues have plagued the United States from

the founding of the country. Over time, many of the

issues have been handled with amendments to the US

Constitution. Others have

been addressed with state and

federal laws to expand voting

rights to more people. Some

believe that a return to federal

oversight to mitigate potential

voter suppression is necessary.

The issues remaining are

often the result of partisanship.

Parties in power can use tactics

such as gerrymandering and

voter suppression to remain

in power. Most voters believe

that their own party wants fair

elections, with 87 percent of Republicans and 83 percent

of Democrats agreeing with this statement. However, only

LAWS THAT HELP PEOPLE VOTE

Over the years, federal laws have expanded voting to many groups of voters. The Uniformed and Overseas Citizens Absentee Voting Act of 1986 guaranteed that members of the US military and citizens that live overseas could register and vote in federal elections. The National Voter Registration Act of 1993 required states to offer voter registration where people apply for driver's licenses. The Help America Vote Act of 2002 required that disabled people have equal access to polling places, voting machines, and privacy to cast their votes.

23 percent of voters in each party think the other party wants fair elections.[11]

There have always been people in the United States working to expand voting rights. These efforts will likely never stop. Additionally, for voters to have the best chance at getting what they want, it is important for them to be educated and informed. They must cast their votes with a good understanding of the issues and candidates they are voting for.

WHAT TO DO IF DENIED A VOTE

People could face problems when trying to vote at a poll. If a voter is in line at the time a poll closes, federal law requires that the person be allowed to vote. Voters should get help from poll workers if the ballots are confusing, if the voter has limited ability to speak English, or if the voter makes a mistake and wants to correct a ballot. Voters who are turned away from voting can report the issue to the Civil Rights Division of the US Department of Justice at (800) 253-3931.

ESSENTIAL
FACTS

MAJOR EVENTS

- In 1870, the Fifteenth Amendment to the US Constitution gives Black men the right to vote by stating Americans should not be denied voting rights based on race. However, in the following decades some nonwhite citizens still struggle to vote because of state laws.

- In 1920, the Nineteenth Amendment ensures the right to vote for women, although in the following decades many Black women still cannot vote due to state laws.

- The Voting Rights Act of 1965 provides federal oversight of civil rights violations in federal elections.

- In 1971, the Twenty-Sixth Amendment changes the voting age to 18.

- In 2013, the Supreme Court overturns parts of the Voting Rights Act of 1965.

- In 2020, the Supreme Court rules that state laws can require members of the electoral college to vote for the winner of their state's popular vote.

KEY PLAYERS

- President Donald Trump was elected in 2016, defeating Hillary Clinton in the electoral college, although she won the popular vote.

- Senator Bernie Sanders, an Independent from Vermont, ran as a Democratic candidate in the 2016 and 2020 presidential elections.

- President George W. Bush defeated former Vice President Al Gore in 2000. He won by 537 votes in Florida.

IMPACT ON SOCIETY

Expanding voting rights in the United States and making it easier for people to vote could make the government more representative of the US population and help the government address the issues that concern the majority of citizens. Some barriers to voting can create socioeconomic inequalities. Additionally, gerrymandering provides a way for those in power to remain in power. Citizens can demand the right to vote and use their votes wisely to make change.

QUOTE

"Voter confidence is a really big thing, and it's the battle I worry about losing."

—*Pennsylvania elections commissioner Jonathan Marks*

GLOSSARY

AMENDMENT
A formal addition or change to a document or law.

CANVASS
To go through a region asking for votes or taking a poll.

COMMISSION
A group that performs the duties of administration or rulemaking for an activity.

CONSTITUENT
A voter or resident of an area who is represented by an elected official.

DISENFRANCHISE
To deprive a group of a legal right.

DRAFT
To require people to register for military service.

INCUMBENT
Someone who currently holds public office.

MANDATE
An official order or commission.

MISDEMEANOR
A crime with less serious penalties than those assessed for a felony.

NATURALIZE
To become a citizen of a country through immigration rather than birth.

NOMINATE
To offer someone to run in an election.

PAROLE
Early release from prison because of good behavior under the condition that good behavior continue.

PROBATION
The release of a prisoner who remains under supervision instead of incarceration.

RATIFY
To formally approve or adopt an idea or document.

SUFFRAGE
The right to vote in a political election.

SUPPRESS
To restrain or prevent.

ADDITIONAL
RESOURCES

SELECTED BIBLIOGRAPHY

Liptak, Adam. "States May Curb 'Faithless Electors,' Supreme Court Rules." *New York Times*, 6 July 2020, nytimes.com. Accessed 7 July 2020.

Parks, Miles. "Why Is Voting by Mail (Suddenly) Controversial?" *NPR*, 4 June 2020, npr.org. Accessed 7 July 2020.

Weeks, Daniel. "Why Are the Poor and Minorities Less Likely to Vote?" *Atlantic*, 10 Jan. 2014, theatlantic.com. Accessed 7 July 2020.

FURTHER READINGS

Anderson, Carol, and Tonya Bolden. *One Person, No Vote: How Not All Voters Are Treated Equally (YA Edition)*. Bloomsbury, 2019.

Harris, Duchess, and Kari A. Cornell. *The Right to Vote*. Abdo, 2018.

Harris, Duchess, and Traci D. Johnson. *Voting, Race, and the Law*. Abdo, 2020.

ONLINE RESOURCES

To learn more about the voting issues of today, please visit **abdobooklinks.com** or scan this QR code. These links are routinely monitored and updated to provide the most current information available.

MORE INFORMATION

For more information on this subject, contact or visit the following organizations:

National Voting Rights Museum & Institute
P.O. Box 1366
Selma, AL 36702
334-526-4340
nvrmi.com
This museum is located next to the Edmund Pettus Bridge, a famous voting rights battleground. It is dedicated to teaching people about the journey for the right to vote.

Women's Rights National Historic Park
136 Fall St.
Seneca Falls, NY 13148
315-568-0024
nps.gov/wori/index.htm
A museum at the Women's Rights National Historic Park tells the story of the first women's rights convention in Seneca Falls, New York, in 1848.

SOURCE
NOTES

CHAPTER 1. A COMPLEX SYSTEM

1. "Second Day." *State Legislature of Alabama*, n.d., legislature.state.al.us. Accessed 4 Aug. 2020.

2. Sam Levine. "Alabama Blocked a Man from Voting Because He Owed $4." *Guardian*, 27 Feb. 2020, theguardian.com. Accessed 4 Aug. 2020.

3. Jennie Cohen. "The Mother Who Saved Suffrage: Passing the 19th Amendment." *History*, 8 May 2020, history.com. Accessed 4 Aug. 2020.

4. Levine, "Alabama Blocked a Man from Voting."

CHAPTER 2. HISTORY OF AMERICAN VOTING

1. Richard Wolf. "Supreme Court Will Hear Case that Could Decide Future Presidential Elections." *USA Today*, 17 Jan. 2020, usatoday.com. Accessed 4 Aug. 2020.

2. Grace Panetta and Olivia Reaney. "Today Is National Voter Registration Day." *Business Insider*, 24 Sept. 2019, businessinsider.com. Accessed 4 Aug. 2020.

3. Panetta and Reaney, "Today Is National Voter Registration Day."

4. "The 26th Amendment." *History*, 27 Nov. 2019, history.com. Accessed 4 Aug. 2020.

5. "The 26th Amendment."

6. Yair Ghitza. "Revisiting What Happened in the 2018 Election." *Medium*, 21 May 2019, medium.com. Accessed 4 Aug. 2020.

7. P. R. Lockhart. "How *Shelby County v. Holder* Upended Voting Rights in America." *Vox*, 25 June 2019, vox.com. Accessed 4 Aug. 2020.

CHAPTER 3. MODERN VOTING ISSUES

1. Martin Kelly. "Presidents Elected without Winning the Popular Vote." *ThoughtCo*, 26 June 2020, thoughtco.com. Accessed 4 Aug. 2020.

2. D'Angelo Gore. "A Short History Lesson on Presidents Winning without the Popular Vote." *USA Today*, 8 Nov. 2016, usatoday.com. Accessed 4 Aug. 2020.

3. "Electoral Votes by State 2020." *World Population Review*, 2020, worldpopulationreview.com. Accessed 4 Aug. 2020.

4. Erick Trickey. "Where Did the Term 'Gerrymander' Come From?" *Smithsonian Magazine*, 20 July 2017, smithsonianmag.com. Accessed 4 Aug. 2020.

5. Michael Taffe. "Democrats Win Majority of Statewide Votes, but a Minority of Seats." *Daily Tar Heel*, 18 Nov. 2018, dailytarheel.com. Accessed 4 Aug. 2020.

6. Samantha Smith. "Voters Have a Dim View of Primaries as a Good Way to Pick the Best Candidate." *Pew Research Center*, 5 Apr. 2018, pewresearch.org. Accessed Aug. 2020.

7. Tom Murse. "Gerrymandering." *ThoughtCo*, 15 Jan. 2020, thoughtco.com. Accessed 4 Aug. 2020.

8. Li Zhou. "Why Iowa and New Hampshire Shouldn't Go First in the Primaries Anymore." *Vox*, 3 Feb. 2020, vox.com. Accessed 4 Aug. 2020.

9. "List of Political Parties." *Ballotpedia*, n.d., ballotpedia.org. Accessed 4 Aug. 2020.

10. Kristina Nwazota. "Third Parties." *PBS*, 26 July 2004, pbs.org. Accessed 4 Aug. 2020.

11. Bill Scher. "Nader Elected Bush: Why We Shouldn't Forget." *RealClearPolitics*, 31 May 2016, realclearpolitics.com. Accessed 4 Aug. 2020.

CHAPTER 4. REFORMS

1. Andrew Daniller. "A Majority of Americans Continue to Favor Replacing Electoral College with a Nationwide Popular Vote." *Pew Research Center*, 13 Mar. 2020, pewresearch.org. Accessed 4 Aug. 2020.

2. "The Electoral College." *NCSL*, 6 July 2020, ncsl.org. Accessed 4 Aug. 2020.

3. "Partisan Antipathy." *Pew Research Center*, 10 Oct. 2019, pewresearch.org. Accessed 4 Aug. 2020.

4. "In Changing U.S. Electorate, Race and Education Remain Stark Dividing Lines." *Pew Research Center*, 2 June 2020, pewresearch.org. Accessed 4 Aug. 2020.

5. Gregory Krieg. "9 Great Quotes about the Iowa Caucuses." *CNN*, 31 Jan. 2016, cnn.com. Accessed 4 Aug. 2020.

6. John Laloggia. "6 Facts about U.S. Political Independents." *Pew Research Center*, 15 May 2019, pewresearch.org. Accessed 4 Aug. 2020.

7. Laloggia, "6 Facts about U.S. Political Independents."

CHAPTER 5. BARRIERS TO VOTING

1. John Laloggia. "Conservative Republicans Are Least Supportive of Making It Easy for Everyone to Vote." *Pew Research Center*, 31 Oct. 2018, pewresearch.org. Accessed 4 Aug. 2020.

2. Laloggia, "Conservative Republicans."

3. Wendy Underhill. "Voter Identification Requirements: Voter ID Laws." *National Conference of State Legislatures*, 9 July 2020, ncsl.org. Accessed 4 Aug. 2020.

4. "Oppose Voter ID Legislation - Fact Sheet." *American Civil Liberties Union*, 2020, aclu.org. Accessed 4 Aug. 2020.

5. Dennis Romero. "Judge Denies Native American Effort to Stop North Dakota Voter Address Rule." *NBC News*, 1 Nov. 2018, nbcnews.com. Accessed 4 Aug. 2020.

6. "Oppose Voter ID Legislation - Fact Sheet."

7. Michael Wines and Alan Blinder. "Federal Appeals Court Strikes Down North Carolina Voter ID Requirement." *New York Times*, 29 July 2016, nytimes.com. Accessed 4 Aug. 2020.

8. Mackenzie Weinger and Elizabeth Titus. "7 Controversial Voter ID Quotes." *Politico*, 11 July 2012, politico.com. Accessed 4 Aug. 2020.

9. Jonathan Shorman and Steve Vockrodt. "Dodge City's Out-of-Town Polling Place Adds to Fears of Voter Suppression in Kansas." *Wichita Eagle*, 26 Oct. 2018, kansas.com. Accessed 4 Aug. 2020.

10. Andy Sullivan. "Southern U.S. States Have Closed 1,200 Polling Places in Recent Years: Rights Group." *Reuters*, 9 Sept. 2019, reuters.com. Accessed 4 Aug. 2020.

11. William Cummings. "'I Wasn't Going to Let Anything Stop Me': Texas Voter Waits Six Hours to Vote on Super Tuesday." *USA Today*, 5 Mar. 2020, usatoday.com. Accessed 4 Aug. 2020.

12. Adam Brewster. "Wisconsinites Brave Coronavirus Fears and Long Lines to Vote." *CBS News*, 7 Apr. 2020, cbsnews.com. Accessed 4 Aug. 2020.

13. "All-Mail Elections (aka Vote-by-Mail)." *NCSL*, 24 Mar. 2020, ncsl.org. Accessed 4 Aug. 2020.

14. Mia Loga. "These States Allow Online Voting for Citizens, Is Your State One of Them?" *eBallot*, 24 May 2018, eballot.com. Accessed 4 Aug. 2020.

15. Max Greenwood. "Turnout Surges after States Expand Mail-In Voting." *Hill*, 7 June 2020, thehill.com. Accessed 4 Aug. 2020.

CHAPTER 6. LOSING THE RIGHT TO VOTE

1. Matt Vasilogambros. "Voting Rights Restoration Gives Felons a Voice in More States." *Pew Charitable Trusts*, 3 Jan. 2020, pewtrusts.org. Accessed 4 Aug. 2020.

2. Grace Panetta and Shayanne Gal. "Floridians with Felony Convictions Are Now Beginning to Register to Vote." *Business Insider*, 8 Jan. 2019, businessinsider.com. Accessed 4 Aug. 2020.

3. "Can't Pay, Can't Vote: A National Survey on the Modern Poll Tax." *Civil Rights Clinic*, n.d., campaignlegal.org. Accessed 4 Aug. 2020.

4. Karen Ridder. "6 Quotes by Ex-Offenders on Restoring Voting Rights to Felons." *Newsmax*, 15 Apr. 2015, newsmax.com. Accessed 4 Aug. 2020.

5. Danielle Lang and Thea Sebastian. "Too Poor to Vote." *New York Times*, 1 Nov. 2018, nytimes.com. Accessed 4 Aug. 2020.

6. "Can't Pay, Can't Vote."

SOURCE NOTES
CONTINUED

7. Kevin Drum. "Thousands of Blacks Are Denied Voting Rights because They're Poor." *Mother Jones*, 21 Nov. 2017, motherjones.com. Accessed 4 Aug. 2020.

8. German Lopez. "Supreme Court's Conservative Justices Uphold Ohio's Voter Purge System." *Vox*, 11 June 2018, vox.com. Accessed 4 Aug. 2020.

9. Roger Clegg. "If You Can't Follow Laws, You Shouldn't Help Make Them." *New York Times*, 22 Apr. 2016, nytimes.com. Accessed 4 Aug. 2020.

10. Sam Levine. "Rightwing Group Pushes Wisconsin Voter Purge that 'Could Tip' 2020 Election." *Guardian*, 18 Dec. 2019, theguardian.com. Accessed 4 Aug. 2020.

11. K. K. Rebecca Lai and Jasmine C. Lee. "Why 10% of Florida Adults Can't Vote." *New York Times*, 6 Oct. 2016, nytimes.com. Accessed 4 Aug. 2020.

12. Panetta and Gal, "Floridians with Felony Convictions Are Now Beginning to Register to Vote."

13. Matt Vasilogambros. "Thousands Lose Right to Vote under 'Incompetence' Laws." *Pew Charitable Trusts*, 21 Mar. 2018, pewtrusts.org. Accessed 4 Aug. 2020.

14. Vasilogambros, "Thousands Lose Right to Vote."

15. Sam Levine. "Voter Purges." *Guardian*, 31 Dec. 2019, theguardian.com. Accessed 4 Aug. 2020.

16. Pam Fessler. "Are States Purging or Cleaning Voter Registration Rolls?" *NPR*, 20 Dec. 2019, npr.org. Accessed 4 Aug. 2020.

17. Vasilogambros, "Thousands Lose Right to Vote."

18. Vasilogambros, "Thousands Lose Right to Vote."

CHAPTER 7. SECURITY AND SOCIAL MEDIA ISSUES

1. Ben Popken. "Election Security Experts Say Hack of Voters' Confidence May Be Biggest Threat to 2020." *NBC News*, 21 Sept. 2019, nbcnews.com. Accessed 4 Aug. 2020.

2. Clare Foran. "Election Experts Say Kris Kobach's Voter Fraud Claims Are Misleading." *CNN*, 8 Aug. 2018, cnn.com. Accessed 4 Aug. 2020.

3. "Elections in America: Concerns over Security, Divisions over Expanding Access to Voting." *Pew Research Center*, 29 Oct. 2018, pewresearch.org. Accessed 4 Aug. 2020.

4. Ron Elving. "The Florida Recount of 2000: A Nightmare that Goes On Haunting." *NPR*, 12 Nov. 2018, npr.org. Accessed 4 Aug. 2020.

5. Sharon Bernstein and Grant Smith. "Ahead of November Election, Old Voting Machines Stir Concerns among U.S. Officials." *Reuters*, 31 May 2018, reuters.com. Accessed 4 Aug. 2020.

6. "Elections in America."

7. Hannah Gilberstadt. "Large Majority of Americans Expect that Foreign Governments Will Try to Influence the 2020 Election." *Pew Research Center*, 12 Feb. 2020, pewresearch.org. Accessed 4 Aug. 2020.

8. Bernstein and Smith, "Ahead of November Election."

9. John Bowden. "Election Officials Concerned by Outdated Voting Machines: Report." *Hill*, 31 May 2018, thehill.com. Accessed 4 Aug. 2020.

10. Peter Suciu. "More Americans Are Getting Their News from Social Media." *Forbes*, 11 Oct. 2019, forbes.com. Accessed 4 Aug. 2020.

11. A. W. Geiger. "Key Findings about the Online News Landscape in America." *Pew Research Center*, 11 Sept. 2019, pewresearch.org. Accessed 4 Aug. 2020.

CHAPTER 8. MONEY IN ELECTIONS

1. "How Much Does It Cost to Become President?" *Investopedia*, 31 Jan. 2020, investopedia.com. Accessed 4 Aug. 2020.

2. "How Much Does It Cost to Become President?"

3. Fredreka Schouten. "A Record $5.7 Billion Was Spent on the 2018 Elections for Congress." *CNN*, 7 Feb. 2019, cnn.com. Accessed 4 Aug. 2020.

4. Chamois Holschuh. "Bernie Sanders: In His Own Words: 250 Quotes from America's Political Revolutionary." *Skyhorse Publishing*, 2015, books.google.com. Accessed 4 Aug. 2020.

5. "The Top 10 Things Every Voter Should Know about Money-in-Politics." *OpenSecrets.org*, n.d., opensecrets.org. Accessed 15 July 2020.

6. Emily Scherer. "Why Democrats Are Falling over Themselves to Find Small-Dollar Donors." *Center for Public Integrity*, 17 Apr. 2019, publicintegrity.org. Accessed 4 Aug. 2020.

7. Tim Lau. "Citizens United Explained." *Brennan Center for Justice*, 12 Dec. 2019, brennancenter.org. Accessed 4 Aug. 2020.

8. Lau, "Citizens United Explained."

9. Dave Gilson. "Bloomberg and Steyer Make Top 10 List of Biggest Super-PAC Donors Ever." *Mother Jones*, 19 Jan. 2020, motherjones.com. Accessed 4 Aug. 2020.

10. "The Top 10 Things Every Voter Should Know."

11. Jonathan Easley. "Largest Democratic Super PAC to Spend $150M This Cycle." *Hill*, 14 Jan. 2020, thehill.com. Accessed 4 Aug. 2020.

12. Dale Eisman. "Poll: Most Americans Believe Our Political System Is Broken." *Common Cause*, 13 Nov. 2017, commoncause.org. Accessed 4 Aug. 2020.

13. NBC News/Wall Street Journal. "Study #18955." *Hart Research Associates/Public Opinion Strategies*, nbcnews.com. 16–19 Sept. 2018. Accessed 4 Aug. 2020.

14. Karlyn Bowman. "A Post-Mortem on Billionaire Candidates." *Forbes*, 4 Mar. 2020, forbes.com. Accessed 4 Aug. 2020.

15. Bowman, "A Post-Mortem on Billionaire Candidates."

16. "Public Financing of Campaigns: Overview." *National Conference of State Legislatures*, 8 Feb. 2019, ncsl.org. Accessed 4 Aug. 2020.

17. "How Much Does It Cost to Become President?"

18. Brad Adgate. "The 2020 Elections Will Set (Another) Ad Spending Record." *Forbes*, 3 Sept. 2019, forbes.com. Accessed 4 Aug. 2020.

CHAPTER 9. ENCOURAGING PEOPLE TO VOTE

1. "The 100 Million Project." *Knight Foundation*, 2019, knightfoundation.org. Accessed 4 Aug. 2020.

2. Adam D'Arpino. "10 Elections Decided by One Vote (or Less)." *Mental Floss*, 5 Nov. 2018, mentalfloss.com. Accessed 4 Aug. 2020.

3. "Remarks by the First Lady at Tuskegee University Commencement Address." *White House*, n.d., obamawhitehouse.archives.gov. Accessed 4 Aug. 2020.

4. "The 100 Million Project: Full Topline Results." *Knight Foundation*, n.d., knightfoundation.com. Accessed 4 Aug. 2020.

5. Jordan Mirsa. "Voter Turnout Rates among All Voting Age and Major Racial and Ethnic Groups Were Higher than in 2014." *United States Census Bureau*, 23 Apr. 2019, census.gov. Accessed 4 Aug. 2020.

6. Nathaniel Rakich. "What Happened When 2.2 Million People Were Automatically Registered to Vote." *FiveThirtyEight*, 10 Oct. 2019, fivethirtyeight.com. Accessed 4 Aug. 2020.

7. "What Is Compulsory Voting?" *International IDEA*, 2020, idea.int. Accessed 4 Aug. 2020.

8. "What Is Compulsory Voting?"

9. "Public Supports Aim of Making It 'Easy' for All Citizens to Vote." *Pew Research Center*, 28 June 2017, pewresearch.org. Accessed 4 Aug. 2020.

10. "The 100 Million Project."

11. Andrew Daniller. "A Majority of Americans Continue to Favor Replacing Electoral College with a Nationwide Popular Vote." *Pew Research Center*, 13 Mar. 2020, pewresearch.org. Accessed 4 Aug. 2020.

INDEX

ABOUT THE
AUTHOR

CYNTHIA KENNEDY HENZEL

Cynthia Kennedy Henzel has a bachelor's degree in social studies education and a master's in geography. She has worked as a teacher-educator in many countries. Currently, she writes books and develops educational materials for social studies, history, science, and ELL students. She has written more than 90 books for young people.

ABOUT THE CONSULTANT

ROBERT Y. SHAPIRO, PhD

Robert Y. Shapiro, PhD, is coauthor or coeditor of several books and has published numerous articles in major academic journals. He is the editor of *Political Science Quarterly* and is the chairman of the board of directors of the Roper Center for Public Opinion Research. His research examines partisan polarization and ideological politics in the United States, as well as other topics concerned with public opinion and policy.